Dr. Eugenie Clark
Swimming with Sharks

Lisa Rao

Contents

Harcourt Achieve

Rigby · Saxon · Steck-Vaughn

www.HarcourtAchieve.com

1.800.531.5015

Young Eugenie's Dream

Some young people dream of being firefighters, baseball players, or movie stars. Eugenie Clark dreamed of swimming with sharks.

When Eugenie was nine years old, her mother took her to an aquarium for the first time. Eugenie looked through the glass at the beautiful fish, then daydreamed about swimming at the bottom of the sea.

"Someday I'll swim with sharks," Eugenie thought. Would her dream come true?

Eugenie had always loved the water. Her mom had been a swimming teacher, and she taught Eugenie how to swim. Whether she was in a swimming pool or in the ocean, Eugenie always opened her eyes under the water. She liked to look at the seashells, the fish, and her own feet.

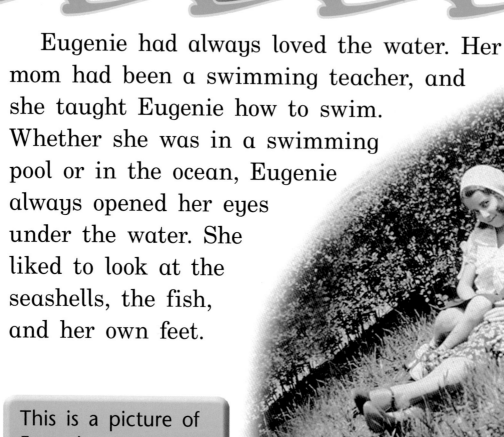

This is a picture of Eugenie as a young girl with her mother.

Even though she loved visiting the aquarium, Eugenie wanted a small aquarium of her own.

One year Eugenie got her own aquarium. She liked to watch the fish swim around the plants, over the rocks, and through the water.

Because she wanted to learn more about sea creatures, Eugenie joined the Queens County Aquarium Society. Members of this group loved to talk about all kinds of fish.

Eugenie's First Diving Adventures

After Eugenie studied sea animals in college, she moved to California. She went to work for a man who studied the activities of different fish. She tried deep sea diving for the first time there.

At that time most divers wore heavy helmets with an air tube that was connected to a boat.

Eugenie had learned that divers tugged on a rope when they wanted to send people a message. People in the boat held onto the rope and felt a tug.

Divers wore helmets like this one when they went under water.

This was the code:

- One tug meant "I'm okay."
- Two tugs meant "I need more rope."
- Three tugs meant "Pull back some rope."
- Four tugs meant "There is danger, so pull me up."

Eugenie put on the helmet and dove down to the bottom of the sea until she could touch the sand.

"Now I'm not pretending anymore," Eugenie thought. "I'm really walking on the bottom of the sea!"

7

One day Eugenie was collecting fish and didn't realize that she was in very deep water. She turned around to see a shark swimming toward her.

Even though she was scared, Eugenie could not stop staring at the shark's beautiful shape. Eugenie's dream of swimming with a shark in the sea had finally come true.

Eugenie swims with a shark for the first time!

9

New Opportunities

In 1949 the U.S. Navy offered Eugenie a job. They asked her to collect and study fish near the South Seas Islands in the Pacific Ocean. One thing that the Navy wanted to know was if people could eat any of the fish living near the islands.

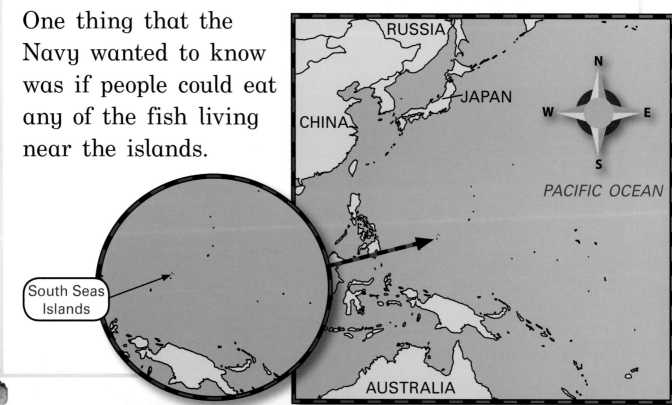

The following year Eugenie tried SCUBA diving. Instead of being connected to the air tube on a boat, SCUBA divers carried their own air tanks on their backs. This was much better for divers because now they could dive deeper. Divers could also stay under water for longer periods of time.

Deep sea divers like Eugenie have benefitted from the invention of SCUBA gear. It helped Eugenie dive to the underwater caves of Mexico so that she could study the sleeping sharks.

11

After Eugenie came back to the United States, she decided to write books about her adventures.

One book was *Lady with a Spear* and it was very popular. Later Eugenie wrote other books and magazine articles, thrilled that she could share her adventures with other people.

This picture is from Eugenie's book *Lady with a Spear.*

In 1955 Eugenie received a phone call from people in Florida who wanted to build a lab. At this lab scientists and visitors could learn more about the sea. They asked Eugenie if she would be in charge of the lab.

She said, "Of course!"

FLORIDA

Gulf of Mexico

lab location

Sarasota

Learning More About Sharks

At the lab Eugenie learned more about sharks. She had always wondered if people could train sharks to do things. Eugenie thought that people would continue to be afraid of sharks, unless they knew more about them. So she tried an experiment. She put a bell in a shark cage with two sharks. Every time one of the sharks rang the bell, the shark would get something to eat. Soon each shark was ringing the bell whenever it was hungry.

Then Eugenie stopped the experiment for three months.

One day she put the bell back in the water. Each shark rang the bell again! Eugenie realized that sharks could be trained by people, and that sharks had very good memories.

Fun Facts About Sharks

- A swell shark can puff up to twice its size so that other fish won't eat it.
- When a shark loses a tooth, another tooth grows in its place.
- A whale shark can have 300 babies at one time!

Eugenie's Visit to Japan

Eugenie received a letter from the Crown Prince of Japan in 1965. He had read one of her books, and he wanted to meet her, so he invited her to Japan.

Eugenie thought of the perfect gift to bring to the Prince. When he opened the gift box, the Prince was probably very surprised to see what was inside of it.

The Crown Prince of Japan invited Eugenie to visit him at his palace.

There was a small shark swimming in the box!

One of Eugenie's friends had made a special box for the shark. The Crown Prince loved his gift.

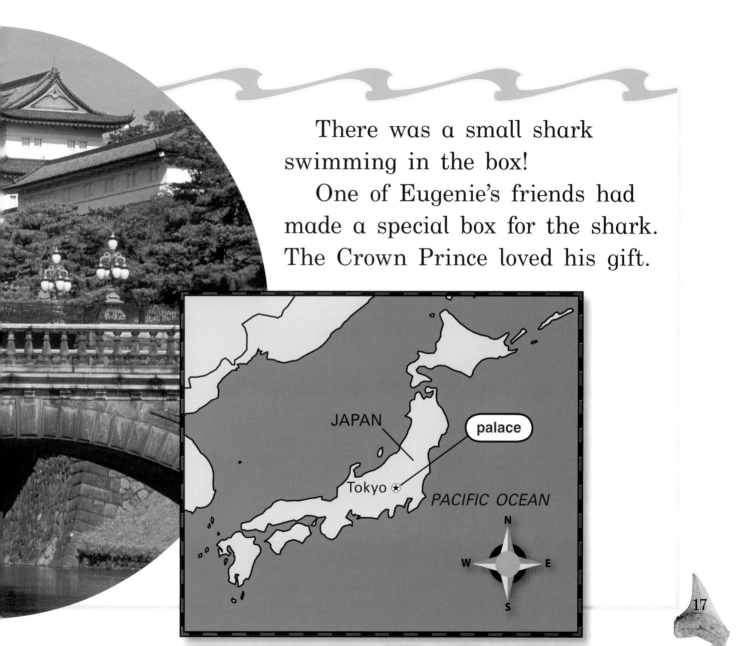

JAPAN

palace

Tokyo ★

PACIFIC OCEAN

Teaching Kids About Sharks

Eugenie has become popular with students around the world. Young people send her questions. They often ask Eugenie if she is afraid of sharks.

Eugenie tells them that she has always been interested in sharks, so she isn't afraid of them. However she also tells people that it's important to understand sharks and to respect them when we dive into places where they live.

Eugenie wasn't afraid to get close to this bull shark.

Eugenie Today

Eugenie loves to share her knowledge with people. She travels to schools, then tells people stories about her adventures.

Some of Eugenie's dives these days are in special underwater boats. These boats allow her to go deeper than ever before so that she can see sharks.

So at age 72, Eugenie hasn't forgotten her childhood dream of swimming with sharks.

Time Line of Eugenie Clark

Eugenie Clark
is born on
May 4.

1922

Eugenie
finishes
college.

1942

1931

Eugenie
visits an
aquarium
for the
first time.

1946

Eugenie
dives for
the first
time.

1949

Eugenie studies
fish in the
South Seas for
the U.S. Navy.

Eugenie writes her first book, *Lady with a Spear.*

Eugenie does experiments to prove that people can train sharks.

Eugenie rides a whale shark.

1953

1958

1981

1955

1965

2004

Eugenie begins working in a lab in Florida.

Eugenie goes to Japan to visit the Crown Prince.

Eugenie continues to study sea creatures around the world.

Index